THE FUTURE OF
BUSINESS INTELLIGENCE

A Definitive Guide on Data Intelligence for
Startups and Enterprises

Elijah Falode

Contents

Preface

By 2025, it is expected that the market worth of business intelligence will have grown to become $33.5 billion[1]. This statistic shows us that business intelligence is making a big impact in the business sector. Unlike before where data collection and analysis was not fluid, simple, and democratic, businesses can now easily maximize data in understanding their markets, knowing the interests and fears of customers, predicting the future, and making effective decisions.

It's not surprising that futurist business owners are, therefore, deliberately acquiring disruptive BI knowledge and tools to position their businesses and corporations in this new intelligence-based era we have found ourselves.

This book, The Future of Business Intelligence, is a reference point for every business owner, manager; sales personnel, IT expert, customer, and other stakeholders who seek absolute knowledge that can optimize the productivity of their business or organization through Business Intelligence (BI).

Every chapter in this book takes the interested reader on a simplified journey that leads to a deep understanding of the concept of Business Intelligence (BI). The contents of this book practically outline the A-Z of data intelligence in businesses and corporations. It doesn't just teach the 'what' and 'why' of data intelligence and business intelligence. It also shows business owners, executives, and every reader how to lucratively adapt and implement data intelligence in their businesses and corporations.

The style, choice of words, and examples are simple, straightforward, and basically what every business owner or stakeholder can relate with. It removes all unnecessary knowledge and illustrations that bore or confuse readers.

The first chapter of this book gives an introduction to data intelligence. It explains the meaning of data intelligence and how it is different from artificial intelligence and business intelligence.

In the second chapter, I shared how data intelligence is improving the efficiency and outcomes of almost every sector and industry. You'll find out that data intelligence is applicable and transforming every industry it finds itself. The all-powerful impact of data intelligence can be seen in business, finance, education, health, travels, entertainment, and many other sectors in the world. No one, no sector wants to miss out on this rejuvenating and profitable touch of data intelligence.

If you're concerned about how your data is managed in a world where secrets and personal information may not really be private, then chapter 3 was written for you. It shows you how your data can be surveyed, manipulated, and used for impersonation. You will learn how businesses are using our data for business gains and why you need to read contract terms both for your personal and business safety.

Read through chapter 4 if you are more interested in how data intelligence applies to your business or corporation. This chapter exposes business owners to the intricacies and significance of Business Intelligence (BI) in their operations. If you're ambivalent about getting a BI tool for data analytics, go through this chapter to understand how it can directly and immensely transform the growth of your business.

Since there's no use learning about business intelligence if we don't know how to implement it, chapter 5 shows you how you can model a BI strategy that will differentiate your business from your many competitors. Chapter 5 is a step-by-step or "hold-me-by-the-hands" guide to creating a BI strategy that works specifically for your business. It sets you a step ahead in the competition and helps you achieve the goals you have set for your business.

Also, in case you are experiencing pressing challenges in your business and you need definite answers to your questions, get a seat somewhere and devour the insights given in chapter 6. These challenges can be: finding it difficult to break even, having poor quality and quantity of data, losing customers, having to deal with an unresponsive market, or even stagnancy. In chapter 6, I discussed and thrashed out these challenges.

Remember that life is a risk and everything we engage in has its risks. It may interest you to know that BI also has its risks. Chapter 7 is about solving every kind of risk that comes with the use of BI. You don't have to worry over the uncertainties and ROI potentials of BI. Just sit down, relax, and implement all the solutions given in chapter 7.

The concluding chapter gives you foreknowledge of business intelligence. It shows you what to expect and the need to position yourself for the future. This kind of knowledge makes you a disruptive futurist because you'll begin to take quality decisions that empower you to dominate your industry.

Everything about this book shows how Business Intelligence (BI) is the present and future of our corporate world. And it encourages every business owner, executive, stakeholder, and team member to actively take part in the high ticket transformation of Business Intelligence.

Chapter 1

What Data Intelligence is All About

It's not surprising that statistically, 53% of business ventures are integrating big data analytics into the core aspects of their business operations.

In our 21st-century information age, overwhelming data footprints are often left for interpretation and utility. Any business that wants to remain floating in its industry must invest in incorporating data analytics tools into its system.

Almost every consumer is now on the world wide web, sharing and consuming lots of information. For a business that seeks and utilizes this available data using analytical tools, data intelligence is the key that unlocks this treasure of useful information that helps organizations make insightful planning and decisions that can improve their quality of performance and improve the bottom line.

So, what exactly is data intelligence?

Data intelligence is simply the use of analytical tools to gather, analyze and utilize the information for a company to gain better insight into their processes, end-results, and consumers' interest. Data intelligence is meant to transform the nature, procedures, and scope of a company's activity in the long run.

With data intelligence, companies can now extract invaluable information which they can effectively use to promote their goals. The metrics used to collect and process data include; consumer interest, business performance, periodic trends, and other information insights.

A New Technology

Our world is constantly evolving to the reality of our imaginations and wants. Also, there is the advent of big data, machine learning, and artificial intelligence (AI) which lead us to an unprecedented future.

Smart machines are not just about the use of synthetic data which does not give sufficient insights into the complex demands of today's world. Smart machines now specialize in the use of 'true' or 'real' data which give insights based on real-time human activities. In this technological advent, data intelligence is a tool that contributes to the processing of information for the profit of business managers.

Data intelligence is an impressive science that has so much promise for 21st-century businesses. It leverages Artificial Intelligence (AI) and Machine Learning (ML). Its goal is to make your products and services more beneficial to consumers while giving you a bulky ROI.

That's why data intelligence software is categorized into five important foundations: descriptive, prescriptive, diagnostic, predictive, and decisive.

The Five Foundations of Data Intelligence

Every business or institution with optimized awareness and utility of data intelligence gets an unusual 360-degree insight into their operations. This knowledge is what makes such business flourish.

The Five Foundations of Data Intelligence are:

1. Descriptive: This is for reviewing the analyzed data to gain a better understanding of business processes and outcomes.

2. Prescriptive: Data intelligence is meant to interpret collected data and proffer alternative or diverse means of carrying out operations.

3. Diagnostic: Data intelligence traces and reveals the causes of occurrences at given times.

4. Predictive: Another purpose of data analysis is to forecast future events and trends.

5. Decisive: Data intelligence uses the information that's derived from analytics to guide decisions and project possible actions.

Every company or individual who uses data intelligence for business or personal reasons understands that data intelligence is like an all-knowing eye that gives users insight into uncommon aspects which they have never imagined.

Since this book is all about explaining the A-Z of data intelligence, let's take a look at another term that's most times confused with it; *information intelligence.*

Does Information Intelligence Have a Different Meaning?

Information is like the gap between data intelligence and business intelligence. It is a branch of data intelligence that offers the transformation of analyzed data into information that businesses can use to maximize the potentials of their businesses.

IGI Global gives a credible definition of information intelligence. It defines information intelligence as: *"the technique of converting big data into useable information for risk management and increased profitability"*.

This definition supposes that with information intelligence, you can extract valuable information from a broad category and streamline, improve, and initiate what's usable into business decisions for greater impact and profit.

What About Business Intelligence?

Unlike business intelligence which is focused on simplifying the meaning of analyzed data for a specific and applied purpose, data intelligence is purely all about broadly analyzing the data gathered (see more in chapter 4).

What's In It For You?

Since we have gained an understanding of the meaning of data intelligence, let's quickly swipe through the importance of data intelligence in our personal lives and the business world.

Here are some of the benefits of data intelligence:

Data Intelligence helps you easily adapt your business to our evolving world.

Our digital world is always changing with new trends and developments. Every day comes with new interests, evolving culture, and new technologies. It now seems like, every day, we are living our dreams of yesterday and becoming familiar with unpredicted events.

Therefore, if your business must stay aloft in this highly competitive landscape, you will have to continually make efforts to understand the times and adapt to the ever-evolving "new". The best way to know what's new and gain an educated understanding is through the insight drawn from data intelligence.

Data intelligence tools help businesses collect and interpret data into solutions to problems of the present. These tools are very vital because they help you spot the trends, understand consumer changing behaviors, and then make profitable adaptations that suit the needs of customers.

Infusing data intelligence into your business operations allows it to thrive in the pressing competition in your industry.

Business owners must always be on the lookout for the new dictates of the market. Through data intelligence, savvy organizations can decipher what customers are thinking, saying, and doing.

Then they can create a trend that leads to popularity. That's why we say data intelligence is very predictive and adaptive to new dynamics and reoccurring patterns.

Data intelligence helps you scale your business faster.

Another benefit of data intelligence is that it gives you the information you need to scale your business faster. You are not left in the dark of what to do. Everything your business needs for improvement becomes transparent to your eyes when data intelligence tools are utilized.

You can efficiently expand your processes, practices, resources when you take data intelligence as a core aspect of your business. This expansion comes with minimal risks and better utilization of resources such as finances, manpower, and time.

Data intelligence gives you valuable insights.

Until you use data intelligence to analyze the big data that runs in your industry and your business, in particular, you can never tell how productive your business is.

The information drawn from big data helps you put forth the best strategy for your business.

You'll know what's missing and what exactly needs to be done to cover this gap. It reveals uncommon and valuable insights that can skyrocket the growth of your business when you apply the result of the report gotten from big data.

Baseline (2014) asserts that just a 10% increase in access to data will lead to a $65 million rise in the net income of a Fortune 1000 company. How remarkable!

Data intelligence shapes the vision you have for your business.

As you may already know, vision is the driving force behind every successful business. However, a vision not well molded to meet the needs of the seasons and the customers will eventually lead to a moribund destination.

Wise analysis of intelligent data gives you an unrivaled and accurate prediction of the future of your business. Your business will have a working long-term plan that makes it outlive the challenges that threaten its growth.

A recent survey by Forbes reports that predictive analysis can increase the ROI of a business by 25%. This is because trends and paradigmatic shifts are identified and reported to the business manager who uses this information to understand customers' interests and psychology, manufacture better products and services, and craft marketing strategies that lead to desirable profits.

Data intelligence builds a solid foundation for big data.

Data intelligence tends to remodel the structure and mechanism of data computation. It improves the quality of big data AI uses. Data scientists, Intelligent BI analysts, BI strategists, Data intelligence warehouse architects, implementation and development experts all have better insights and optimized capabilities with data intelligence.

Data intelligence helps you segment and profile customers.

This function of data intelligence is what gives clarity as you serve your customers better. It helps you as a business manager or marketer to understand your targeted customers and 'remarket' to them effectively.

Data intelligence is very impressive in grouping consumers according to their purchasing behavior, common interests, demography, preferences, and many other placements. All of these data offer every business owner the knowledge they need to provide for their customers only what they want.

Data intelligence helps you understand your business investments.

The sole purpose of data intelligence is to help organizations make informed decisions.

If you are wondering whether your business is giving you a reasonable amount of profit, the best way to cure your worries is through the utility of data intelligence. With intelligent analytical tools, you can investigate the rate of progress of your business and therefore tell if your business is accruing profit or loss.

Not only can you detect the profitability of your business, but you can also project the outcome of future investments with data intelligence. Unlike before, there is now minimal risk in investment once the proper analysis is carried out with data intelligence. It guides you on the best areas you should invest your finances and resources. And it shows you how to go about it.

Data intelligence helps you in planning and logistics.

Your organization can now have a more efficient way of doing business when data intelligence is used. There's optimal scheduling of events, the optimal location of warehousing, better delivery times, and identification of potential external factors,

Conclusion

Data intelligence is now taking its place in the world of technology. It has risen from a point of obscurity to one of the most relevant aspects of big data and information technology. And it's still unveiling so many promises to man and his society. Data experts and entrepreneurs are working hand-in-hand to search for more opportunities that data intelligence can give to our present and future society.

In the next chapter, we will specifically highlight how data intelligence directly affects our personal lives and businesses.

Chapter 2

Data Intelligence in the Real World

Having looked at what data intelligence is about, we now understand that this modern concept comes with so many benefits when applied to different sectors correctly.

In this chapter, we'll take a peep into the operations of data intelligence in real-life situations; and in various sectors and industries. Here are a few of them:

Education

It's been said that "Education is the weapon which we can use to change the world" (Nelson Mandela). Well, as education is doing a service to the world, we are in turn giving back to education for its development through data intelligence.

As one of the world's most important and biggest sectors in the world, it's absolutely interesting to see that data intelligence is now affecting education positively.

Unlike before where educators find it difficult to keep track of students' records, transformational educational systems have been able to curtail this setback through data intelligence. Educators can now provide interesting and effective learning experiences based on the information gathered from data intelligence.

This information is usually fed into AI systems in a bid to provide a more beneficial and qualitative dimension of teaching and learning situations.

Educators don't have to worry about historic or foundational data of students again. Data intelligence tools are now available for educators to monitor, diagnose, and predict both teachers' and learners' behavior and performances.

Educators are equipped with a comprehensive view of learners' past, present, and future experiences for greater impact.

From Luan Hui et al (2020) research, the application of data intelligence in education can be traced back to about 50 years ago. To our benefit, it is getting more advanced annually. This system of data intelligence in education was initially called Intelligent Tutoring System "SCHOLAR" and it was originally made to make the learning of geography effective.

Most research on AI for education development has focused on intelligent tutoring centers, chatbox, and robotics. This is a shift from the early days of data intelligence.

In Luan et al findings, Big data of students are now massively available on diverse platforms such as social media (Facebook, Instagram, Twitter, etc), Online learning platforms (e.g Udemy, Coursera, etc), learning management systems (LMS), and intelligent tutoring systems (e.g AutoTutor).

All of these are providing an increasing amount of data that contain the physiological data, personal records, and learning performances of students. To become useful, these data are interpreted with learning analytics which is the collection, analysis, and reporting of data of learners to help educators understand the learners and optimize learning environments. Machine learning and AI are sometimes used to process the information derived from data analytics.

Data intelligence will feed educators with enough information for the planning and designing of a curriculum that's contextually suitable for learners. It enhances teacher support, methodology of teaching, and assessment of students. It gives teachers more accuracy in predicting the outcome of students and the provision of personal learning.

As for the learners, the metrics for measuring the impact of data intelligence in their lives are level of performance, interest in schooling, and learning outcome.

Travels

With the help of data intelligence, the travel industry has been able to use data in predicting people's reasons for travel, when they'll like to travel, their most desired needs, and how to meet these needs with the best pricing and customer service.

Travel providers use the deductions from analytics to identify when travelers have a high or less demand for tickets. Then they adapt their facilities and offers to meet the needs of their customers.

Strategies are revamped and applied. Processes and policies are amended accordingly when new pieces of information are derived from the data of customers; therefore leading to optimization of customers' satisfaction and growth of the business.

Airline

Most airlines all over the world face so much loss in profit. They find it difficult to maintain a profitable occupancy ratio. With the help of data intelligence, airline service providers now know how to minimize costs and maximize profit. They can now predict a delay in flight take-off, whether to arrive at a destination or halt halfway, or create programs to entice more customers, etc.

Healthcare

The healthcare sector is one of our dearest and revered sectors in our economy because it's the place where life and death decisions take place. The right treatment or decisions will lead to elongation of life while the wrong treatment or decisions may result in the termination of life.

In the healthcare industry, there's always the need to analyze contextual and complex data set to enhance the decisions taken in the hospital or healthcare facilities.

There are several ways in which healthcare analytics and data intelligence tools have impacted the industry. One of them is seen in the hospital dashboard system.

Durcevic S. (2019) reveals that the key performance indexes of the hospital dashboard system are: patient wait-time, ER wait-time, and treatment costs.

It's not unusual to see inefficiencies in traditional healthcare facilities. This situation is because a lot of data are transferred from one department to another and this often leads to fragmentation or incomplete data.

Fortunately, the hospital dashboard provides a comprehensive overview of all data in a central location. This technology leads to improvement of service and efficiency in the healthcare industry.

Gone are the days when so much unnecessary work was needed just to organize, process, and store patients' records. In the modern-day, there are Electronic Medical Records (EMRs) which use data intelligence to store the medical information of patients on a central platform. With this innovation, medical practitioners can have access to patients' complete records from anywhere and without any hassle.

Data intelligence has also played a big role in the invention of fitness sensors and wearables which help individuals take care of their health.

Individuals don't have to visit the clinic all the time for a check-up. Everyone can now monitor their health with these devices enabled by data technology. Medical professionals can monitor their patients' health from afar. They are immediately notified once there is a threat to the health of their patients or when there is an emergency.

Search Engines

Have you ever wondered how search engines like YouTube, Yahoo, Ask, Binge, Google suggest the complete title of what you are searching? We sometimes feel like these search engines have been "spying" our thoughts because they seem to accurately know what we want. These search engines use data intelligence algorithms to determine frequently searched phrases that are related to what you are typing in the search bar.

Retail

The retail sector is the world of demand and supply. Before the advent of modern data intelligence, data had always been used to study consumer behavior for marketing purposes. However, the introduction of data intelligence into business has improved the productivity and profitability of the retail sector.

The impact of data intelligence on the retail sector can be seen in the retail dashboard where the primary KPI are: average units per customer or average transaction size. This platform gives insight into the recurring behavior of consumers, values, and orientation. It shows retailers the products that are most popular and preferred. This kind of priceless information is what makes technological savvy stores get bigger and better with sales.

Online Shopping

It's amazing how e-commerce stores such as Amazon can suggest products that are similar to what you want. Online shops use customers' data to study their preferences and shopping records to give a customized experience to every customer.

In a massive pool of products and services, this makes online shopping easy and efficient for customers.

Finance

Banks used to experience debt, losses and so many customers' complaints when data intelligence was not used in the finance sector quantitatively.

Companies in the finance sector are now able to accurately analyze past expenditures, profile customers using variables, predict and manage risks. These companies now leverage the use of data intelligence in the prevention of fraudulent practices that are common in the financial sector.

Banks can now effectively identify and provide a solution to credit card fraud and breaches using data intelligence tools. Customers' data are now more secured than ever before.

Logistics

We can see the role of data intelligence in delivery companies such as UPS, FedEx, DHL, etc. Data analytic tools are used to improve the quality of services rendered to customers. The result of this improvement is absolute trust, loyalty, and patronage of these logistics companies. We are certain that our deliveries will be made at the exact time and location we desire. This efficiency is possible because of the deep insight derived from data analytic tools.

Digital Marketing

The digital marketing industry is one of the biggest users of data intelligence. The digital billboards you see and the ads on websites are all effective because of the algorithm of data intelligence. As a digital marketer, you can directly target your customers who are mostly interested in your products and services.

You can reach out to customers based on their demography and past behavior such as preferences, purchasing power, education, marital status, employment, etc. Digital marketing is easier and highly targeted than traditional marketing. Companies that focus on traditional marketing are now fusing digital marketing tools into their operations.

Speech Recognition

Life seems to be getting easier every day. We are increasingly switching from manual to automatic methods of doing things. We are now in a tech world where we seem to live by the idea of "say it and have it done". Speech recognition inventions such as Cortana, Siri, Google Voice are gaining much popularity and usage every day. With the speech recognition feature, you don't need to type the keyboard or swipe through your devices anymore. Your car and other intelligent devices can be operated using the speech recognition software which functions with data intelligence.

Face recognition

When face recognition was at its early stage, its level of accuracy was not too excellent. Face recognition devices are used to find it difficult in differentiating faces from objects. Similar faces were not easily distinguished. And even the authentic faces were sometimes identified as fakes.

The sophistication of data intelligence has made face recognition better than its earlier versions. Face recognition devices can now tell the difference between a smile and a frown. Law enforcement agencies in advanced societies highly use data intelligence software in their operations to reduce the crime rate.

Entertainment

The impact of data intelligence on entertainment is ever increasing. It is seen in platforms such as Netflix and Spotify. These platforms use data intelligence to give users of these platforms ease in choosing what movie to see or the music to listen to.

Netflix as both an entertainment and business platform makes use of customers' data insight and viewing habits to upload movies that its targeted audience will want to watch. The use of data intelligence also helps Spotify in customizing your music playlist.

Gaming

The gaming industry is getting more sophisticated every day. Game developers such as Nintendo, Zynga, Sony, EA Sports, etc use data intelligence to create more appealing gaming experiences which will satisfy the cravings of users.

As a player proceeds to a higher level, the game adapts and upgrades itself using machine learning algorithms.

Weather Forecast

Satellites are situated across the globe to provide an accurate weather forecast. These satellites gather so much data about the environment. They study the weather patterns and use the information derived to predict future occurrences. Environmentalists use data analytical tools to ascertain the level of climate change and forecast natural disasters.

Safety in our Society

Data intelligence plays a major role in law enforcement, traffic, risk management, and many other aspects that ensure safety in society. Most crimes are now more predictable and traceable than ever before.

Conclusion

Data intelligence is winning our hearts as the days go by. Its impacts are palpable in every sector of our world. Indeed it's transforming not just businesses but also our individual lives.

However, it is no news that ethics and privacy are big issues confronting the collection and utility of data intelligence. In the next chapter, we'll take a thorough review of how companies manage our private data and what the implications are.

Chapter 3

Ethical and Privacy Issues in Data Intelligence

Are our data sold or exposed to third parties without our consent? How much do we suffer when there are data breaches? How much of our privacy is maintained? Are our identities safe in the hands of companies that use data intelligence?

All these are questions we ask ourselves every day. As much of our data are captured, analyzed, and stored, we want to know if privacy is dead. It's humane to be cynical about what data analysts are doing with our data.

Although we already know that the concept and use of data intelligence are very impactful in our society, we are, however, worried over how almost every intelligent device and website captures our data; both at home and in the public.

In this chapter, we'll be looking at how data is collected and analyzed using artificial intelligence and data intelligence. It briefly explains the meaning of privacy, it reveals how privacy is endangered, and it shows you how your data is used.

Privacy Defined

Privacy in its simplest definition is one's right not to be observed (Bartneck et al, 2020). And humans always seek some level of privacy in their dealings. Naturally, humans maintain privacy in different ways. This can be in form of putting on less revealing clothes, closing the doors, speaking in hush tones, and many other ways that promote privacy.

We value our privacy for so many reasons. Some of these reasons are:

1. It makes us take decisions without the pressure that comes with the idea that someone is watching us.

2. It helps us to be very analytical in our interactions with others.

3. It also allows us to make decisions that are not socially acceptable. That's why anonymous forums seem to have the most expressions of the dark or shady aspects of human behavior.

The State vs the Citizens

However, as individuals claim their right to privacy, governments all over the world do all they can to have more access to the private affairs of their citizens. Governments are of the view that less probing or maximal access to citizens' vault of data is directly proportional to an increase in the level of crime rate. They argue that law enforcement agencies need as much private information as they can to prevent and reduce criminal activities in society.

In contrast, people have never been willing to find this proposition of invasion of privacy meaningful. This is mostly because of the three reasons for privacy earlier mentioned in this chapter.

In the United States, for instance, the laws about privacy rights are very flexible and susceptible to change to the demand of the court's judgment. How much privacy you have is subjected to context. Age, mental capacity, geographical area, nature of the case, are some factors that determine how the United States Supreme Court grants privacy to citizens.

The Dilemma of Businesses

In the battle of what's obtainable in the privacy of citizens, we find out that most companies choose to maintain a neutral position. Most of these companies are themselves flexible. In a situation where the government uses pressure, these companies use discretion to determine if they should or shouldn't protect the privacy of the customer and bow to submit to the demands of the government.

However, it's a known fact that Apple is one of those few companies which do not grant government agencies access to locked iPhones. According to the company's policy, it doesn't matter whether the information will be useful to the government or not. Their priority is the privacy of their customers. (Holpuch 2016).

The companies which are so adamant about not giving in to government pressure believe that customers will only continue to patronize them if they truly feel that their data is safe.

However, those companies which surrender to the will of the government usually do this because they are persuaded by the fact that they'll surely need the government's support in policymaking, legal obligations, and other favors.

It's also interesting to know that customers don't usually have a totality of privacy. As much as companies try to make customers feel that their data is secured, these companies use these data for marketing purposes; although with the consent of customers who are told to read and "agree" to the terms and conditions which most customers seldom read thoroughly.

Facebook for instance uses data intelligence tools to profile customers and help digital marketers use targeted adverts to reach specific customers whom their products or services are most suitable.

That's why when you like or engage with the post of a page on Facebook, you are probably going to start receiving adverts from this website or page. The system has learned that you have some level of interest in that page. So, the company or owner of the page can start directing their products and services specifically to you. Fortunately, you may find some of these ads useful.

The Prevalence and Dangers of Data Collection

The collection of data in our society today is far easier than any time that has ever existed before now. Intelligent technologies such as surveillance cameras, PCs, smartphones, the internet, etc, have made it extremely easy to create, process, and store information.

Almost all our activities leave footprints of us and can easily be tracked. The photos we upload on social media give away our location, time, and other pieces of information. Other times we fill online forms and much of this data are stored in the cloud.

Whenever we upload our information on social media sites like Facebook, Instagram, etc, we are often sharing copyright to the providers of these platforms which may decide to use the data or sell it to third parties without our express consent or royalties.

Google is one of the biggest collectors of users' data. It takes note of your interest any time you search for a topic or term in its search box. Your most private or intimate desires are collected whether you know it or not.

Now the questions that rest in the hearts of users are: how safe is my private data? How do I regain control over the information I push online?

The honest answer to this question is that users have little control over their data. These online platforms are businesses whose major goal is to make a profit. And access to your data is what gives them the opportunity of achieving this goal.

It takes telemetry data of a vehicle's performance and reports back to the manufacturers. This information is used to identify distances covered, understand the overall performance of their products, and make improvements.

Digital Assistants: Tools for Persistence Surveillance?

Personal Surveillance is a continuous observation of a person or thing to gather information. This concept is common in the military or security intelligence agencies. What many don't know is that persistence surveillance has now been domesticated.

Digital companies like Amazon and Google use their digital assistants to monitor and gather information about customers. Google's Voice Assistant and Amazon's Alexa are typical examples of products that carry out persistent surveillance.

Using data intelligence, these systems stream the audio data of users from the home or office back to the manufacturers' database where it is collected, analyzed, and stored. In theory, these products can be secret agents which observe and capture users' data without their knowledge.

To counter these theoretical assertions, Amazon has tried to convince users that its products have limited capabilities. It claims that the wake-up word "Alexa", helps limit when and what information its products could process.

However, Wikileaks has some proof from NSA documents which shows that theoretically, some backdoor vulnerabilities or loopholes of these devices can be exploited for persistent surveillance.

Also, on the issue of persistent surveillance, there's another significant example: the "Hello Barbie" doll. This product uses speech recognition software, speech synthesis, and conversation management to function. The targeted customers of this product are young girls who wish to converse with a "pet" and share their personal experiences such as their joy, pains, and struggles.

The cause of concern is that in these conversations, a lot of private information is shared. The manufacturer, Mattel, assures users that their data are highly secured and their privacy protected. But the questions cynics ask are: what about the uncertainties? What will be Mattel's privacy management scheme tomorrow? Are there vulnerabilities hackers or third parties might manipulate?

This situation makes customers unsure of what to decide about these products. Digital assistants are amazing and sophisticated tools that make life more comfortable yet their privacy is threatened.

Drones: Tools for Persistent Surveillance?

Unlike digital assistants, citizens do not personally install this surveillance equipment to watch over them. Originally, they were meant for warfare: to study battle models, observe the enemies, and predict attacks. In recent years, drones' usage is not limited to warfare, they now have domestic use. For example, Baltimore installed over 700 cameras around the city in 2005 for ground surveillance. It was called CitiWatch (Bartneck C. 2020).

Since then, it has expanded its program in providing security through persistent surveillance of the city. When citizens were asked in a poll about how they felt about being surveyed, 82% of those who answered the Baltimore Business Journal stated that they were comfortable with the innovation since the purpose is to ensure their security and their privacy is respected.

The Cockpit and Privacy Issues

Airline authorities have consistently sold the idea of streaming live audio from the cockpits of airplanes. It sounds like an objective and logical idea because there won't be much need for retrieving black box recorders. However, pilots have also consistently resisted this idea because it threatens their privacy in the cockpit.

Manipulation of Private Data

Most times users are not fully aware of how their private data are processed, stored, and sold to third parties. The non-intended or unethical utility of users' private data is a big issue facing the world of data intelligence.

We can see how ads are successfully programmed to speak directly to us and to affect our psychology. Adverts are so specific that we can't help buying these marketed products or services. The tremendous specificity of these ads has reversely made some potential customers develop an anti-adverts mechanism. Instead of making instant purchases, they resist the urge with speculations and distrust.

The fact is we have not yet fully dug into the depth in which data can be manipulated at the back-end. For instance, there was the Cambridge Analytica scandal in 2018. It showed how data gathered through an online platform like Facebook can be used to manipulate election outcomes.

Artificial intelligence software and social robots can manipulate the views of the populace, especially in socio-political milieus.

Privacy and Impersonation

As we give laudable applause to AI technology, it does not yet negate the fact that AI through data intelligence can be used for impersonation. In speech recognition, it was discovered that the Adobe VoCo system could imitate the exact voice sequence of a person after listening to a conversation for 20 minutes.

Another manipulative impersonation through privacy is seen in revenge pornography. Vengeful partners can go to the extent of manipulating porn videos and placing their ex-partners' faces. Using neural networks to create deep fakes, this act is usually done to tarnish the image of a personality before the truth is discovered.

Unread Contracts

Do you always take out time to thoroughly go through the contracts or terms of an agreement on apps, software, and online platforms? It's quite rare. And it's not our fault anyway. The

Terms and Conditions are usually too lengthy or boring to study. So, we just scroll through and click the "I agree" or "I accept" or "sign up" button. Most times, it's because we are more interested in the benefits than the consequence of our ignorance.

So, we are ready to take the risk of our privacy and hope that if the policy will truly nail us down, someone, maybe an activist, out there will take out time to read through the privacy policy and take legal actions against the platform; if need be.

As we have earlier mentioned, Facebook and Google own all the pictures, messages, and videos we upload on their platforms. And, every day, we can see how they indirectly sell our data to digital marketers who target us with their adverts.

In 2018, The General Data Protection Regulation (GDPR) in the European Union established that companies must directly seek the content of customers before selling off their private data.

The question remains: how many times has your consent been sought before your data is sold or used? And do we have a choice to say no? Imagine not using Facebook because you are not comfortable with the policy and after much thought you realize that most of what you do is deeply integrated within the platform.

The Privacy of the Vulnerable

The violation of privacy can affect the vulnerable population in different ways. When we say the vulnerable population, we are simply referring to the children, the elderly, the sick, and those who can't help themselves.

It's of utmost importance that the data generated on patients' health are kept private. This data can be physical and mental health, family genetics, personal setbacks, death prediction, and other forms of limitations. This set of information is to be maximally protected, not to be discussed or directly referenced without the express consent of the patient.

But if we are to ask out of curiosity: how well can we believe that the so-called health experts do not casually discuss some of these data with family members or friends; when they ought to be one hundred percent confidential?

Older adults' mortality can be predicted with gait information technology (White D. K. et al, 2020). This technology studies the movement of a person and theoretically predicts the death date of a person. If data privacy is not respected, a business-centric individual might carry out a mass survey, identify prospects whose mortality is almost due and proceed to sell them funeral packages.

An Ambivalent Situation

Privacy continually remains an issue of ambivalence. Humans want to enjoy both privacy and comfort whereas we can't always be sufficiently convinced that our privacy is fully respected.

A large number of the population may be willing to give up their privacy if they are offered great benefits and a soothing hope that their privacy is protected. In contrast, there are still some citizens who do all they can to resist the utility of devices or platforms that threaten the safety of their privacy.

Will we ever have true privacy?

The rate at which the private data of individuals are violated daily calls for more customers' awareness and legal actions. What raises more concern is that most customers do not care or are ambivalent about what to do in the situation. They want their privacy and they also want the benefits of the products or services. They seem to be at crossroads.

As we litter the online world with our data, we should bear in mind that the internet is watching, gathering, storing, and predicting our next moves whether we are aware or not.

Chapter 4

Data Intelligence for Businesses and Corporations

We have explored the meaning and usefulness of data intelligence across various sectors. We've seen that data intelligence is also impactful for businesses and corporations.

But if you are still curious and asking: what more can my business derive from data intelligence? Are there some other things about data intelligence I need to know?

Yes, there are so many benefits to gain from data intelligence in your business or corporation. And this chapter is meant to unzip the intricacies of data intelligence for your consumption and future implementation.

What again is Business Intelligence?

In the first chapter, we had a brief definition of business intelligence (BI) and promised to expand in this chapter. Now let's get on with it:

Business Intelligence (BI) is a combination of data tools, data mining, data visualization, business analytics, and infrastructural resources to help businesses make logical, comprehensive, and profitable decisions.

To know if your business is leveraging business intelligence, simply ask yourself: are we mining customers' data using data intelligence tools? How much are we gathering customers' data to improve our business strategies?

These questions are the first steps to discovering if your business is using data intelligence for your corporation.

Business intelligence is a tool almost every organization uses either passively or actively. As you might guess, advanced and lucrative businesses are heavy users of business intelligence. The veins of their activities are embedded in the use of business intelligence because they've consistently seen the impact it has on their revenue report. Business intelligence helps business managers have a comprehensive view of data within their organizations. It shows them how to filter inefficient resources, adapt to new market demands, and take active actions to drive change.

Business intelligence entails the processes of collecting, analyzing, and storing data derived from internal and external business operations to add appreciative value to the system. When all of these items are brought together, then business managers can have an omniscient view of business activities and make productive decisions.

According to CIO Africa, Business intelligence (BI) makes use of software and services to collect, organize, analyze, and simplify data for gaining insights into useful insights that can help businesses make strategic decisions.

These pieces of valuable information are prepared and presented to stakeholders as summaries, dashboards, charts, graphs, maps, and illustrations. With this information, stakeholders can fully understand the performance of their business without guessing.

What's the True Value of Business Intelligence?

Seeking to know the value which business can bring into your business is what we call due diligence. CIO Africa highlights four fundamental reasons why businesses and corporations use BI and why you also need it:

1. Corporations use business intelligence to keep a record of employees' data and improve retention rates in the organization. It helps the business manager determine how best to improve workers' productivity, compensate them, and increase retention rate.

2. Business Intelligence tools are used to track sales and delivery of products and services. It

gives insight on what products and services are more desirable, what should be optimized, and what should be terminated.

3. With BI, sales team managers can identify the level of sales performance of each team member and address issues that will improve sales.

4. Great BI enables businesses and enterprises ask and answer questions about their data.

Business intelligence can assist companies make informed decisions by revealing the present and historical data within their business context. Some ways in which business intelligence(BI) can help your companies make smarter, data-driven decisions are to:

- Discover ways to improve bottomline
- Analyze customer behavior
- Compare their data with competitors
- Track performance
- Optimize operations
- Predict success
- Spot market trends
- Discover issues or problems

The Big Fours of BI

How do we identify true BI? What are the things to expect from a BI tool? As you think of becoming one of the fans of BI, it's proper you know the significant features of BI. This knowledge will fine-tune how many expectations you have for BI.

Scheps S. (2008), groups BI features into four; calling them BI's Big Four. XYZ explains that BI insights are supposed to be accurate, valuable, timely, and actionable.

Accurate Insight

Most decisions you take are based on the quality and quantity of information that is available to you. The collected and analyzed data ought to be accurate. That's, it should be true and useful to the objectives of your company. The accuracy of information matters a lot in decision-making. Therefore, any BI tool that does not give accurate information is to be suspended or ditched.

Scheps reveals that the BI tool is like other technological tools. It works with the Garbage In, Garbage Out principle. That's, an inaccurate BI insight will lead to limited or wrong decisions while accurate BI insight is more likely to lead to better insights. Let's say the BI insight inaccurately shows that there are poor sales in a particular market or place. The manager might take decisions that are not helpful because of the wrong information they are working with.

And when team members produce accurate results using BI tools, then stakeholders should trust the report and run with it. Nothing is as frustrating and discouraging as having one's accurate work disregarded for personal reasons.

Even if there's a need to question the accuracy of shared results, it should be done professionally. You have indeed been working hard yet data insights are saying otherwise. At the surface level, things may look alright. But at the deeper level, so much wrong might be tangling the processes.

That's why BI tool developers do their best to make sure BI technologies are very dependable. These tools should be what users can trust every day. If their results are not accurate then what's the need for a BI?

Valuable Insights

Scheps also mentions that BI is not just about giving accurate information. It's good to have accurate information but what if such information does not bring any taste or significance to your business? This kind of performance makes us want to say "go to hell" to the BI tool. We look to BI to give us insights that will not just be accurate but also impactful in our businesses. We need valuable information that will give our customers satisfaction and increase profit.

Timely Information

When reports are given after decision-making minutes, there will be no impact. Stocks and crypto are traded with the help of business insights. If these insights are not accessed on time, they lose value.

Bad timing can be a result of some sort of delay which may be hardware or software problems, logistics issues, or human excesses.

Actionable Conclusions

Any insight that is illogical or beyond the scope and strength of a business is as good as useless. If, for example, BI insight accurately reveals that the key stakeholders will have to step down for your business to go up, we call this non-actionable conclusion. It's not something that can easily be done.

Therefore, a BI tool should not just produce accurate, valuable, or timely information. A BI conclusion should also be actionable.

Processes of Data Intelligence

The meaning and processes of business intelligence continue to evolve every day. These processes are according to Tableau:

Data mining: Data mining is a core aspect of business intelligence. It is the use of machine learning, databases, and statistics for the discovery of trends.

Reporting: This stage of business intelligence is the sharing of processed data as valuable information to the stakeholders of a business. It helps the stakeholders make informed and savvy decisions that can impact their bottom line.

Performance Metrics: At this point, the stakeholders through the assistance of the data intelligence department within the organization compare current performance with past data. Goals are measured and adjustments are made.

Descriptive Analytics: Data analysis of stored and processed data is fetched to describe the causes of problems and provide solutions.

Querying: This point simply entails asking or querying the data with specific questions which business intelligence answers through the data stored in its database.

Statistical Analysis: The result of descriptive analysis is further analyzed or interpreted to determine what's trending and the cause of the trend.

Data Visualization: Analyzed data are also transformed into visual representations such as bar charts, histograms, graphs, for easier description and interpretation of data.

Visual Analysis: Data is explored using visual storytelling techniques to give insights into the process of the flow of analysis.

Data Preparation: This process involves compiling data from vast sources, measurements, and preparing the outcome for analysis.

Every business has its specific targets such as the type of employees it wants, the revenue and profit to be made annually, rank in its industry, quality of review/feedback from customers, and many other goals. The use of business intelligence helps businesses achieve this goal with profitable decisions taken.

Businesses also have unanswered questions which business intelligence provides answers to.

BI Strategy

In time past, Tech experts were the main users of data intelligence and BI technologies. The technicalities made BI inaccessible to the masses. It was secluded for IT professionals who had the means and wits for carrying out analytics and understanding the outcome. However, BI has evolved to become accessible to the masses. The tools are more simplified and user-friendly.

Classic BI Vs. Modern BI

In classic or traditional BI, data experts utilize in-house data on transactions for description, prescription, and prediction. Organizations often rely on classic BI when the goal is to produce an accurate result using standard and predictable data. That's why financial reports are usually carried out with classic BI

In modern BI, however, businesses use data from an intuitive system for analysis. Typically, modern BI tools are used when a business urgently needs to gain insight that will disrupt the current system and prescribe a dynamic strategy. Modern BI is used when speed is valued over accuracy. Modern BI is used if the projected outcome, such as the quick penetration of a market, is what matters to the business user.

As essential as strategic BI is needed for the growth of a business, many organizations still find it difficult to implement. This is basically because of poor knowledge and utility of data.

Self-service Business Intelligence

As business intelligence receives wide popularity, there has become a need to make business intelligence tools available for the masses that have little or no knowledge of technical jargon. Businesses can now carry out business intelligence processes on their own. Although IT experts will always be needed to take on complex tasks, they are not necessary for the basics. Do-it-Yourself (DIY) or self-service tools are now available for business owners or non-technical staff.

Sometimes, a thorough understanding of these tools will demand some training which employees and business owners can easily learn. To encourage non-technical staff to come on board, business owners will have to make the advantages obvious.

The downside of depending on self-service BI is that your organization might end up with a mix-up of metrics across departments, generate inaccurate reports, fall into data security issues, expose vulnerabilities, and some other unforeseen challenges. It's alright to use DIY or self-service BI. But to do this perfectly, you'll have to employ experts to train your team. You'll also need these data professionals to work with you when complex issues arise.

Software and Systems for Business Intelligence

Within the business sector, there are different data intelligence software and systems business owners can use to serve their customers better, minimize cost, and maximize profit. According to Tableau, this software usually have the following features:

• Dashboards

• Visualization

• Data Mining

• ETL (Extract-Transfer-Load; which is used to import data from different sources).

• OLAP (Online Analytical Processing).

• Reporting

SelectHub identifies that the most popular of these features are dashboard and visualization. They present data reports in simple, direct, and summarized form. They are value-oriented; that's, they usually give a comprehensive view of business analytics results.

Out of the multiples of software available in the data space, these are some of the popular ones:

Microsoft Power BI: This is a tool that enables you to master business intelligence and leverage the Power BI toolsets. It covers important concepts such as installation, creating data models, building basic dashboards, as well as visualizations so you make informed business decisions

Tableau: This is a DIY or self-service analytics platform which provides data visualization feature for users. You can integrate with other software or applications such as Excel and Microsoft Azure Data Warehouse.

Splunk: It's a great platform because it provides users the feature of guided analytics.

Alteryx: This platform combines analytics in diverse sources to make workflow within the system simpler and rich in the provision of insights.

Qlik: This platform is effective in business intelligence, business analytics, and data visualization. It provides extensive insights into the gathered and analyzed data.

Domo: This platform uses cloud technology. Its utility is effective across diverse industries. It provides specific business intelligence tools to industries such as health, finance, education, business, etc. It's made for CEOs, IT experts, employees, and even sales representatives.

Dundas: It's mostly used for creating scorecards and dashboards. It can also be used for either ad-hoc or standard reporting.

Google Data Studio: This is an advanced version of Google Analytics. As a business owner or CEO, you may want to try it out for your organization.

With these software, businesses can easily study and understand precisely why sales are low, high, or static. This information helps business managers or board of directors come up with more effective business strategies that can bring in torrents of benefits.

Business Intelligence (BI) and Business Analytics, any difference?

Though both technologies function together, they are not the same thing.

Business intelligence is descriptive. It shows the business manager the present situation of things and the past events that led to the present situation.

On the other hand, business intelligence is predictive. It uses data analytic tools to project what will likely occur in the future. This projection can be in the near three months' time or a distant ten years. Through business analytics, businesses can be prepared for future trends.

Business analytics is also prescriptive. It shows businesses what they need to do to stay productive. It identifies deficiencies within the structure and system of a business. Then it provides a working solution for them.

Business analytics is more like data analytics. The difference is that business analytics is centered on businesses while data analytics is applicable in diverse sectors.

Also, the difference between both terms is not just in the past, present, and future capabilities. It's more than that. Business intelligence and business analytics are also different in respect to the person who is in charge of handling the processes or who it's meant for. Data scientists carry out business analytics and interpretations while business intelligence gives a comprehensive and simple to understand report to the business manager.

The Symphony of Data Analytics and Business Analytics in Business Intelligence

Business intelligence uses data analytics and business analytics in organizing, computing, and interpreting data. Business intelligence helps users understand all the data analytic jargon. After the data analyst has made known his findings, he or she passes the information so that business intelligence can perform its role of creating useable models for the business owner.

Business analytics is a tool organization used for data mining, applied analytics, statistics, and predictive analytics. It's a bigger strategy of business intelligence that organizations use to improve questions on the query.

Business analytics is more critical or in-depth because it accepts the fact that queries shouldn't be linear because the outcome will be illogical or unrealistic. Answering a question often leads to more questions or iteration process of exploration, discovery, and information sharing. This is defined as the analytics cycle; a concept which explains how businesses react to changing questions through the help of business analytics in business intelligence.

Data Visualization and Visual Analytics in Business Intelligence

Humans are naturally visual in creation. We perceive and collect a large amount of information using our sense of sight.

We have a better appreciation and interpretation of data that are represented in ways we can see and associate with our minds.

Data visualization tools are used to interpret visual data for business utility.

Visual analytics helps you have a clear understanding of data analysis. It's a common and effective way of presenting business intelligence. Visual analytic tools convert data into understandable visual sets such as graphs, charts, and other forms of illustrations. Data visualization tools are used to interpret visual data for business utility.

Major Industries and Business Intelligence (BI)

Industries across sectors are vigorously adopting business intelligence. These industries include healthcare, education, entertainment, and the many industries identified in chapter 2 of this book. All businesses in these industries can apply data intelligence for transformation.

For example, Tableau tells of Charles Schwab which offers financial services uses business intelligence to have a panorama view of results across its different branches in the United States. This exercise helps the organization take the measurement and identify a resourceful area of strengths and opportunities.

Branch managers can now keep track of clients' needs because this will surely affect the direction of growth and quantity of investment. The General Manager can investigate the performance of managers across the regions. Business intelligence helps managers understand who is doing well, what he or she is doing, and plan towards making unbiased promotion or in the awarding of outstanding employees. In the long run, both the business and clients will benefit from this decision.

Conclusions

Diverse industries such as entertainment, retail, finance, oil, and much more are adopting business intelligence in their activities. This evolving situation is not just because these business managers want to feel like they are part of the trend. It doesn't seem so. Everyone wants BI simply because of the overwhelming impact business intelligence has on their businesses. It allows users to understand customer behavior, predict and scale profits, repair vulnerabilities, and many other benefits that come with the utility of business intelligence.

In the next chapter, we'll look at how to use business intelligence to create a business model that brings in maximal benefits.

Chapter 5

Creating a Business Intelligence Model

Business Intelligence has proven to be like an elixir that revives the processes and achievements of businesses. Every modern business needs analytic tools to convert raw data to useful information. But knowing the "what" of business intelligence will not take you to the destination you seek. You need to also know "how" to implement data intelligence. You need to learn how to create a model or strategy that can sustain your business.

In this chapter, we'll discuss the significance of business intelligence strategy. And for us to truly appreciate these models, let's take a peep into the "why" or purpose of creating a business model.

Why Do You Need to Create a Business Model?

A Business Intelligence Model or strategy gives you a blueprint, direction, and means of solving data problems. It structures your organization's activities and helps it stay focused.

Before we buttress how to create an effective model for your business, let's take a look at the elements of business intelligence strategy which Alexsoft has outlined:

1. Vision: You must ask yourself: why am I using business intelligence for my organization? What do I want to achieve? When do I want to record this achievement? What will be the impact of this achievement?

2. People and System: You should define the human resources involved. Who do you intend to serve? Who are the people you need to carry out your vision? What processes will give you valuable outcomes?

3. Structures and Tools: You need to identify the analytical or intelligence tools which will be most beneficial for the vision, people, and system you are modeling for.

From the order of the elements, we can see that your company's vision will lead you to the kind of people you work with, the method or process these people will work with, and the tools or software you use to achieve this goal.

Now, let's walk through the steps you should use in creating an effective BI model for your organization. Altexsoft (2020) identifies the following steps for setting up a BI strategy or model.

Step 1: Observe What's Already Existing

Before you can get to your destination, you must understand where you are coming from. Take a look at what you already have (or don't have). Be objective about tools or software that have been productive, those not relevant, and those that are not available. You need to be thorough and clear about this assessment.

To get a solid and comprehensive result in this internal assessment stage, you may need to invite stakeholders, managers, BI experts, employees, and go through customers' feedback.

You'll have to ask pertinent questions such as:

What's our BI vision? Do we have any at all? What do we hope to achieve? Which strategy will align with this vision?

Are we getting professional advice? What's the trend in BI? What are we missing? How do we leap?

How are we managing data? Do we have the right hands on deck? What tools are we currently using? Are these tools efficient enough? Do we have the license?

It's at this stage you carry out SWOT analysis. This analysis will help you identify your assets, liabilities, and problems.

After concluding step 1, you can proceed to stage 2 of creating a model for your business.

Step 2: Create the Vision

Your vision is a well-stated purpose that gives your business direction. You need to know what you want before we can proceed to search for how to arrive at this destination. Your vision helps you make the right decisions. It's the road map.

It shows both stakeholders and employees the purpose of their roles and encourages them to use the right analytical tools.

Your vision for BI should identify the head of BI operations, how your BI model aligns with the company's goals, how the organization will support BI processes, and the infrastructure you'll need to implement the vision.

Step 3. Choose a BI Platform

The wrong BI platform or tools can adversely affect the final results or expectations. Your platform must align with the vision you have for your business. Here are some features to consider:

• Data interaction in the dashboard or visual interface

• User-friendly and self-service system

• Giving deep insights and discoveries

• Open for collaboration and data sharing with others.

Step 4. Set up BI Governance Team

BI governance simply means the process of identifying and using the BI infrastructure or tools that have been established. It includes three fundamental components which are

A. BI governance team

B. BI Tools and Lifecycle Management

C. User Support

A. BI Governance Team:

In establishing BI governance, you'll have to choose team members, identify their functions, and state the work atmosphere or relationship that's permissible. It includes everyone that is connected to the business; that's the executives, the employees, and the users. It's not just about the IT experts or those at the bottom of the ladder. BI governance encompasses everyone.

Nonetheless, some large businesses will prefer to have a BI governance team that comprises experts only. These experts may include data scientists, programmers, and experts in relational databases. This kind of group is not cheap to hire. But it's worth having.

B. BI Tools and Lifecycle Management

BI lifecycle is the architecture or framework which gives support to BI efforts. This structure starts from the data sources (External, ERP sources, etc). Then it proceeds to the data integration process where data is converted and taken to the repository (such as data marts or data warehouse). After this, you can now see the data displayed on the dashboard or any interactive tool.

This involves choosing a BI tool, creating the process of data integration, presentation of data, and training of personnel.

C. User Support

You should make feedback processes available. User support helps you understand the problems of those who ought to benefit from your BI model. To give appealing support to users, then you should provide data education support, tool support, and business support.

When you are done setting up the BI governance team, proceed to road map design.

Step 5: Create a Road Map

Your road map is a visual presentation of what's obtainable at the various stages of implementation. When creating a road map, you highlight tasks and set a time frame for achieving them.

It contains implementation steps that are carved from the vision and knowledge of available BI tools.

After mapping out a model or how to carry out your strategy, the next thing you should do is documentation.

Step 6: Document Your BI Strategy

A BI strategy document is the tangible road map that leads the organization on what actions to take at certain times. It usually takes the following format:

A. Executive Summary: The executive summary is what you write last; though it comes as the first section in your document. It's an overview of what you intend to do, the model you are using, and the time frame you wish to fulfill this target.

B. BI benefits and problems: Write out how this model will benefit your organization, the possible problems you may encounter, and the solutions.

C. Scope and Resources: In this section, you outline your scope or targeted audience. State the resources you'll need to drive through the road map up to the final destination. These resources include staff, budget for architectural design, and cost of acquiring customers.

D. BI governance team: Clearly outline your BI governance team and their positions.

E. Alternative models: In this section, you show users likely alternative means that'll lead to an impasse. Explain why they are futile roads and your audience will have confidence in your model.

F. Evaluation: Highlight the metrics for calculating success.

G. Appendices: Provide additional information such as bibliography, glossary of terms, charts, etc.

Step 7: Review Your BI Model Annually

You can either use quantitative or qualitative metrics to understand the maturity level or profitability of your business. Using both will be more effective. An annual review helps keep track of your ROI and other dynamics of business. It helps you know what's working, what needs to be improved, and what needs to be ditched.

Conclusion

Your BI Model pioneers everything you desire to achieve using business intelligence. It's similar and as important as creating a business plan for your business. An absence of a BI Model in business that uses BI is like heading to a destination without a clear idea of how to get there. This kind of journey only leads to a lot of bumps, falls, trials, and errors. Every BI business should get a road map using a well-drafted BI model.

Chapter 6

Business Problems with Data Intelligence

From what we have learned in previous chapters, Business intelligence (BI) tools harmonize the data derived from marketing, sales, and finance, to provide real value that culminates in improved product and service delivery.

The solutions business intelligence (BI) offers to businesses outweigh the cost of implementation. It solves cumbersome and small problems most businesses face. In the long run, business intelligence gives more benefits than expenses.

Exe software identifies the following as some challenges you can effectively resolve when you use BI tools for your business:

1. You have insufficient or poor data.

This situation usually leads to the inability to predict, prescribe, or diagnose processes that'll lead to the growth of your business. Without accurate and sufficient data, you find it difficult to control your business processes.

The process of gathering, analyzing, and storing data in Business intelligence is dependent on the quality of data you have in your ecosystem. To resolve this challenge, you'll have to gather fragmented data which may include:

• Data from advertisement

• Data from website analytics

• Contacts, sales, and requests data from CRM

• Offline data.

To have reliable data, you'll have to audit the channels or sources of the data with BI tools. These data will be cleaned up before they are stored. This vetting process solves the problem of insufficient, inaccurate, or poor data. It assures you that the data is both reliable and valuable for your business.

2. Your revenue data from online and offline sources differ.

The reports from Google, YouTube, Facebook, and banner advertisement campaigns often tell how great or abysmal the result is. However, instead of feeding on these reports hook, line, and sinker from marketing agencies, why not take a look for yourself using simple BI tools.

To know what's the profit value of each revenue source, you'll have to create an individual attribution model using BI tools. This framework will help you determine your actual cost and the revenue obtained from each source. It shows you where your leads are coming from, their purchases, your audience interests, and how to engage them.

3. You are finding it difficult to manage different ad campaigns.

BI tools help you understand how to manage the impact of each campaign in your ad system. It helps you in delisting unprofitable funnels and providing real-time value to customers. We can say it's the solution to your dwindling business and uncountable expenses. BI tools help you determine the cause of your limitations and help you plug in the solutions that lead to the right solution. This solution may be as simple as focusing on converting existing leads into purchasing customers.

4. Your business seems to be stagnant.

There is a point in your business where you struggle to rise beyond the status quo. All your efforts on advertisement and old strategies seem to be ineffective. At this point, it's recommended you give BI intelligence a chance. A BI tool will trace the problem and prescribe the exact solution you need.

5. There's poor business performance or outcome.

Business performance is one critical aspect of a business. It determines how long the business will survive in its niche. But what happens when you discover that your business has red ink marked over it? How do you revive a business with poor performance?

The answer to this lies in using a BI tool in your business operations. BI tools give you access to insightful analytics on the root of poor performance and how to tackle these causes. Data intelligence helps you make meaningful decisions that add long-term value to your business. You have a daily tracker on the performance of your business. It helps you gain an immediate idea of what curve your business is taking. It helps you spring swiftly as you resolve the poor performance issue.

When this business problem is proactively resolved, you can proceed to deal with other challenges which BI can efficiently solve.

6. Your market is unresponsive.

This is the same as losing so much money while you worry helplessly. BI insight allows you to know what's trending and support you with ideas that will help you meet market demands. It shows you what products and services you need to stop producing and how to position your business for maximum profit.

You'll be able to decisively upsell and cross-sell products your prospects will positively engage with. When you utilize data intelligence for your business, you have a chance of standing out in the competition.

Data intelligence also helps you to correctly respond to unprecedented situations which may threaten the growth of your business.

7. You are losing customers.

Entrepreneurship is basically about making an impact and profit. If any of these two indices are missing, then there will be no equilibrium in the socio-economic ecosystem. Business intelligence helps you understand your customers' behavior. It shows you why they are not buying, what they want, and how to get them their desires.

Customers are humans. And humans love to associate with people who understand their fears, needs, and joys. With BI tools, you can create more personalized services that will solidify a quality relationship between your business and your clients.

8. You are faced with neck-breaking challenges when running the daily affairs of your business.

These difficulties can come in form of entering data on spreadsheets, sales performance, calculations, and other day-to-day affairs in the workplace. Business intelligence is a unifier that simplifies collaboration among business tools, departments, and operations.

BI tools help you integrate diverse processes and reports in one central location. Data is transformed into easy-to-understand documents so that both technical and non-technical staff will have access to the results of day-to-day activities.

9. You are merging multiple systems rather than analyzing data.

It's alright to expend time and energy in the sourcing data from different channels or platforms. The problem is that many organizations focus more on data collection from diverse sources than data analytics.

When you appropriately use BI tools for your business, there's a synchronization of data. All of your data can be accessed from a single dashboard. This symphonic integration of things makes business easy and efficient in operation.

10. You are over-dependent on IT Experts.

Some businesses prefer to use complex traditional data tools. The problem with these tools is that they make you over-dependent on tech experts. Without their expertise, you'll find it difficult to operate the system.

This is a problem that can be solved with the use of modern BI tools. These tools are custom made and every top personnel can understand and operate these tools.

They help you save time and cost used in consulting expensive tech experts. These simplified tools also give you some degree of relief because you and some other staff can directly derive information from analytics.

This democratization of BI tools has led to more acceptance and utility of data intelligence in businesses.

11. You're struggling to keep up with demands. So, you need speed and accuracy in your business.

The globalization of technology in today's world has brought extreme ease to our way of life; especially in our businesses. Computers are now mini-mobile devices we can use for high-tech functions. Business managers, executives, and other staff members can now access, share, and utilize data comfortably.

This development, to which BI belongs, breaks so many barriers and leads to better and faster decision making. Through BI, you can take your business to the top.

Conclusion

Our world has evolved to the extent that everything we do in business has been oversimplified. Problems which were once resource-consuming are not as such anymore. Businesses that use data intelligence have better chances of improving their products and services, giving better offers, and getting greater ROI than their competitors.

Data intelligence provides growth opportunities for businesses and solutions to burdensome business problems. It provides a win-win situation for both businesses and customers. Businesses accrue significant profits while satisfying the needs of customers.

Chapter 7

Risks in Business Intelligence

We have talked so much about business intelligence (BI); to the extent that you may want to dive in immediately. But before you join the "BI users club", it's important you know the entirety of what you are signing up for. Business Intelligence is not all glitz and glory.

Business intelligence has its risk. And this is not strange because life itself is a risk. All we can do is manage the risk and hope for the best. In this chapter, we'll take a look at some of these risks and their solutions. Here are the most common ones:

1. The result of your BI tool may not meet up your expectations.

Every business manager has big dreams and when the promises of BI are set on the table, we are tempted and quick to go for it. Unfortunately,

BI tools may at times work like magic but it's not magic. Just like every man-made tool, BI tools may not always yield our desired results.

This situation often arises when so much has been hyped about the potentials of a BI tool. When reports and analytics don't match with expectations, there's a loss of confidence in the necessity of BI. Since this is a risk we all have to bear, here are some steps we can take to bring out the best of our BI tools:

- Be realistic about your goals. It's not easy to attain goals that are unrealistic or beyond the level of planning and resources. So, forget the mighty promises and stick to what's achievable.

- Before you purchase your BI tools, do your homework. Search for the best vendors. Seek sincere reviews and referrals.

- Ask for a product demonstration and be sure that it fits your business goals. Have an open dialogue about the features of the BI tools.

- If possible, seek a guarantee. After the vendor has shown you a proof of concept, request a guarantee or availability of an adequate support system.

2. There's a temptation to cross the line.

Sometimes, sales may shoot up and truly your BI technology over-delivers. This is good news, right? Isn't this the positive outcome of our risk? Sure it is.

However, the problem with this kind of good news is that you didn't prepare for the windfall. You'll be tempted to push beyond your scope. You can't help quickly setting up a new BI strategy to meet up these increasing demands.

To resolve this problem and turn this outcome in your favor:

- Plan for the best. Business is all about risk and opportunity management. Think of every possible outcome so that when they come, you'll be over-prepared to handle them. Be accountable for every data request, data collection and analysis, unexpected cost, and customers purchases.

- Say no. If the surging requests are far beyond your scope or vision, you may have to say "no". It's better to say "no" than take a risk that leads to underperformance and the tarnishing of your company's image.

3. Not everyone is willing to adapt to the 'strange' advancement.

It's quite unfortunate that business managers and BI teams may be enthusiastic about the BI project whereas the end-users or populace are not dazzled. You find out that only very few want to use the BI tools. The others are stuck with the old; not willing to make changes.

Savvy business owners now take surveys before purchasing a BI tool. This is because we have seen how employees and top managers resist change. Some workers see this sort of advancement as strange and a hindrance to the system they are used to. This dilemma makes managers cautious of the introduction or adjustment of a BI system. Managers try to bring everyone on board because it'll be a big loss if the population shows gross aversion towards the new technology.

To bring everyone on board, do the following:

- Explain to team members how the BI tool will assist them in their functions, increase productivity, and achieve the company's vision.

- Raise awareness before the introduction is made. Show the non-technical staff the features and benefits of the BI tool. You can keep the change slow and steady.

- Consider the end-users before acquiring a BI tool. Ensure that it's a tool user can adapt to.

- Before and after the launch of a BI project, consistently provide training and support for users. Help them see the current perspectives of BI.

- Monitor users' utility of the BI tools. Are they comfortable with the change? Have they fully accepted the new technologies? What are their fears? What are their struggles? You'll need to observe and provide answers to these questions. If you can do this early, you'll be able to curtail every negative objection before they become critical.

4. Your BI tool needs to stay current.

Nothing is static. Everything around the workplace is bound to change. Your company's vision, culture, atmosphere, and demands will surely experience some levels of change. This situation calls for BI data models, data sources, and scope to continually remain in a state of flux.

As a business manager, you must always look out for these changes and ensure your BI project aligns with the company's goal. Your BI solution must always describe and reflect the present realities.

The best ways to attend to this risk is to:

- Plan ahead for a change.

- Evaluate every phase, quarter, or season of your business to identify the current needs.

- Any BI tool, data source, or model that does not meet up with the new changes and needs should be dropped for another.

4. There is the poor quality of data.

Poor management of data often leads to poor data quality. Your source of data and the process of analysis need to be kept clean before launching out. When there's no proper data management, the final report is usually poor in quality. After the disappointment, users and sponsors may lose faith in the BI tool.

The solution to this is:

- Create enough time to prepare your data. Don't be too quick to launch your BI project.

- Have a regular data management plan. Be deliberate about seeking to know the quality of data you are gathering. Don't leave this to chance.

- Invite experts to test the usefulness of data sources and data models. Will the derived information be impactful? Will it positively bring value to your company? What is lacking in the data source?

Conclusion

As it's said: it will be wrong to 'throw away a baby and the bath water. There are indeed some risks or challenges businesses face when adopting BI or trying a BI project. This shouldn't, however, deter you from looking at the brighter side and resolving these challenges which have been discussed in this chapter.

In the next and concluding paragraph, we'll take a step into the future and see ahead what BI promises to offer our businesses and corporations.

Chapter 8

The Future of Business Intelligence (BI)

B usiness intelligence continues to win the hearts of business executives. BI tools are seen as keys to a world of possibilities. Business owners can now specifically identify the needs of their customers. Then decisively proffer the best products and services that suit every customer.

Today's world of business is unlike before where managers seem to be walking in a dark alley without any sure idea of the consequences of their actions. Businesses now have access to the data of consumers. They now know the thoughts, words, and fears of customers. Based on inference drawn from past and current data, business managers can now accurately predict the future actions of their customers.

And in all of these impacts and challenges that tag along, we are left wondering: if the past could have led to this admirable present, what will the present lead to? What is the future of business intelligence? Will there be some dramatic changes? How many returns are we to expect from future BI? What new risks will future BI present to business owners?

The answer to all of these curiosities is found in this chapter. Taking into consideration these predictions will equip you for tomorrow. It will differentiate your business from your competitors. You'll be miles ahead taking steps they have not thought of and having higher ROI.

To understand what beholds data intelligence in your business, let's eavesdrop and peep into the secret of future BI.

Collaboration in Business Intelligence

Many experts like Conrad (2021) have predicted how BI tools and BI platforms will be more collaborative. Most BI tools function independently in the digital world. Users do not often connect these tools to broader networks.

However, experts forecast that users and systems will have greater integration than we have ever seen.

In the article titled The Future of Business Intelligence (BI) in 2021, Conrad quotes Brian McKenna who predicts that: in the future, BI experiences will be more immersive and shared among users. Teams will be able to efficiently collaborate in real-time as they use handy devices. Stronger Teams with Analytics and Artificial Intelligence, and that businesses are merging machine learning systems and other forms of data intelligent tools are leaping on with strides and making a huge impact.

This collaborative effort is already happening and it promises to get bigger.

Data Visualization

With data visualization dashboards like Domo, users will be able to predict the present and future needs of customers. Businesses will be able to spot 'unactualized' gold mine trends and ride on the benefits before the crowd becomes aware. Data visualization will help businesses make better budget planning as they identify the goose that lays the golden eggs.

More of Self-service through Machine Learning

BI software will become more intelligent than we have ever imagined. This will reduce dependence on external factors and give room for self-service. This form of intuition will not just be based on pre-programmed intelligence but the kind that is contextual and adapts to new changes. A business intelligence tool will be able to answer questions that demand an understanding of the multiplicity of contextual factors. Through machine learning, solutions will be more customized than programmed.

Managers will be able to ask intelligent software questions that normal machines won't have been able to "reason out". Data intelligent software will have access to knowledge that is beyond their boundaries. Machine learning systems will give meaningful answers to thoughtful inquiries by searching through past and present big data.

Data proactivity is simply information brought to you without human effort. Business intelligence processes will function smoothly even with your passivity. There'll be no need to go to the dashboard or opening a report book. All of these will come to you through data proactivity.

Advancement of Data Networks

As data intelligence continues to dominate the business sector, swathes of data are processed. More advanced networks and structures are developed to adequately accommodate this surge of data.

For example, we can see how cloud technology is receiving increasing utility. Businesses and individuals patronize cloud service providers which offer storage and data management services. Cloud engineers and data scientists are working tirelessly to provide advanced hardware architectures. This advancement will allow users to have storage, secured, and quality management of the massive amounts of data.

Apache and Amazon are examples of companies that are active participants in the business intelligence revolution. They offer architectural support to business intelligence strategies.

Prescriptive Analysis

Although using data intelligence to predict occurrences is not new in the business world, there will be more accurate forecasts and utility of BI for this purpose. BI will not stop at making predictions. It will also make suggestions for setting up profitable strategies for the future.

Natural Language Processing (NLP)

Don't be surprised when you see NLP playing more roles in businesses. Information and business processes will be more simplified through BI. We see them in the chatbox and customer service. But expect more advanced functions of NLP soon.

Automations and Augmentation

We are just starting to scratch the surface in the use of automation and artificial intelligence for businesses. More sophistication should be expected. Through augmented analytics, data will be expressly analyzed, reported, and shared for utility and feedback. Users will be able to get deeper insights into their modus operandi.

How to Position Your Business for a Data-Centric Future?

The thriving business of the 21st century is that business that understands the past satisfies present needs, and be well-positioned for the opportunities that are in the future. To tackle the demands of our present reality and prepare for a promising future, many businesses look to the features of business intelligence. No wonder the business intelligence market evaluation is on a leap to the moon.

But to maximize the full potentials of BI, your team and strategies will have to be data-driven (using the methods in chapter 4). You will have to integrate a data-centric culture into the workplace. Define your vision, your goals, and inspire your team to commit to it. Clearly state how business intelligence will improve the quality of your product and services and yield a higher return. Show your team members why and how you can use business intelligence to your advantage.

According to Thelosen in Conrad (2021), the components that make up a data culture are grouped into three. They are a bottom-up and a top-down commitment to BI analytics, and education.

A bottom-up and top-down approach to business intelligence comprises the commitment of every team member. Lower management should involve business intelligence in their day-to-day activities while upper management should utilize BI tools for analytics and decision making.

Business owners should ensure users are educated on the handling of BI tools that are becoming more user-friendly. Everyone is not on the same knowledge level; especially when it comes to the use of technology. Therefore, everyone must be given specialized training on the use of BI tools and be shown how these tools directly affect the growth of the business.

Also, every business which desires to partake in the future of business intelligence should be ready to acquire infrastructures and BI assets. The business of tomorrow is for those who are prepared to conquer the data-driven future.

Conclusion

Business intelligence will be more meaningful, faster, automated, insightful, user-friendly, and personalized in the future. There will be more collaborations and free flow of data within the workforce. Early and heavy users of BI technologies will dominate their niche and create the trends which their competitors will have to live up to.

Other Books by the Author

Microsoft Power BI Demystified

 Whether you are a business owner, data analyst, or financial analyst, you would like to collate data easily, analyze it, and share some with your colleague in real-time. You would want to do this with software that is easy to operate and publish data with good visuals in a way that you can understand. Microsoft Power BI allows you to get data from different sources, analyze it, and gives you insights into your business and operational performance. You can share workspaces with your colleagues, and they can easily access the business reports you have prepared. It makes collaboration easy. In this book, you will find out what Power BI is, the features, the benefits, and the functions.

This book also discusses the different versions of Microsoft Power BI – Power BI Server, Desktop, Pro, Premium, and Report Server. You will get to understand the diversity between these versions, their features, benefits, and how to set them up. You can operate these Power BI versions both on cloud and on-premise, depending on the features of the versions. You can also share your workspace with as many people as you want. You will get to understand the Power BI versions, and which one best suits your company's needs.

Power BI also allows you to inquire about your data and gives you answers to your question. This is due to the artificial intelligence feature. It also provides you the insight you need to make informed decisions that impact your company's bottom line positively. Microsoft Power BI can also integrate with other on-premise apps on your device to enable you to collate data easily. It operates with natural language so that you won't need the help of an expert to operate it.

If you are looking for advanced software that is better than your Excel, Power BI is the upgrade you need. This book will guide you on everything you need to know about Power BI, and it gives an easy step-by-step guide on how to install, setup, and use it.

The Future of Intelligent Automation

Since the 1800s, automation has been assisting humans in taking up roles in different industries like finance, travel, healthcare, education, and different sectors of life. This invention has developed to what we now see as intelligent automation because of its major capacity to learn and adapt to novel situations through a process called deep learning. Today, intelligent automation is performing amazing roles and making life much easier for us.

Intelligent automation is deployed for tasks such as customer care, fraud identification, teaching, and facial recognition. Because it's making so much impact in today's world, we're tempted to seek the future of automation.

The future of automation is roped with the certainty of robotic software, not just being automated but intelligent. The future will have humans engaged only in major roles such as programming, creativity, and supervision because automation has become highly intelligent enough to finish up simple and complex tasks.

When you read the first chapter of this book, you'll understand how automation has evolved over many years to become what it is today---intelligent software. It is now about machines that can understand their environment, interact, work with humans and other machines, and even learn from personal experiences.

In the second chapter, I explained the concept of intelligent automation in the simple and understandable way.

Chapter three clears the air between similar and complementary technological concepts; intelligent automation (IA) and artificial intelligence (AI). It gives you an insight into how factors such as machine learning, natural language processing, predictive analysis, and robotics are combined in new technologies. An example of this complementary invention is driverless cars, which use numerous inventions such as **sensor inputs**, **camera feeds**, historic archive, and **real-time machine feedback** to give a comfortable and **secured driving experience** that you've never had.

If you stop to read in chapter three, you may not capture a very peculiar aspect of intelligent automation, which you'll find in chapter four. It discusses the effect of automation in industry. You'll understand how automation helps in the customization of products and services, reduction of production or delivery cost, and improvement of efficiency. In marketing, for instance, offers are personalized according to clients' profiles and choices, while automation is resourceful in identifying and putting a stop to fraudulent transactions in credit card processing. Intelligent automation has become so useful in industries that you can hardly picture a bank without ATMs or a store without a POS. It is now an important aspect of most industries in today's world.

The trends of intelligent automation are highlighted in chapter five, while the pitfalls of intelligent automation are explored in chapter six. Some of the pitfalls of intelligent automation include overspending, allowing artificiality to reign over natural intelligence, trying to automate everything, and replacing humans outrightly, and some other adoption mistakes which every knowledge seeker on intelligent automation needs to read in chapter six.

In the last chapter, I recollect how intelligent automation will be the mainstream tool of the future. And there will be more advanced intelligent automated software in the future. These machines will possess a higher degree of adaptability features and an unprecedented level of productivity and value propositions.

This book is like the manual and scripture of intelligent automation because its content reveals everything we currently see of intelligent automation and what to expect in the future. It's informative material for every individual, group, or company that desires to take the lead in its sector. If you are one of the few potential successful persons who want to have a share of the future before others begin to scramble for the crumbs, then follow me as I take you from the first to the last chapter of this automation scripture. Read more or order your printed copies here>>

About the Author

Elijah is an expert content writer and a sought-after ghost-writer with over ten years of experience in content development around emerging technologies, digital marketing, and publishing. He studied Education (Economics) at the Obafemi Awolowo University (class of 2012) and presided over the Campus Entrepreneurship Initiative (CEI).

In the past five years, he has collaborated and worked with thought leaders and industry experts across the globe as a content development consultant. He has authored other books which include Microsoft Power BI Demystified and The Future of Intelligent Automation.

He currently mentors over 100 leaders on how to build a successful freelance career. He also has a passion for producing content that can help small businesses and large enterprises get paid, seen, and heard on the internet. He is happily married and blessed with two adorable daughters. You can connect him on Linkedin @Elijah Falode

Bibliography

Altexsoft (2020) Retrieved from https://www.altexsoft.com/blog/business-intelligence-strategy/ on 7th March 2021.

Amazon.com. Is Alexa Listening? https://www.amazon.com/is-alexa-always-listening/b?ie=UTF8&node=21137869011

Austin R. (2019). The invention of voice recognition, this century's phenomenon. Retrieved from https://www.cio.com/article/3400238/the-invention-of-voice-recognition-this-centurys-phenomenon.html on 4th March 2021.

Bartneck et al (2020). Privacy Issues of AI. Retrieved from https://link.springer.com/chapter/10.1007/978-3-030-51110-4_8 on 5th March 2021.

Bartneck C. et al (2020). An Introduction to Ethics in Robotics and AI. 1st Ed. 2020. https://www.amazon.com/s?k=9783030511104&i=stripbooks&linkCode=qs

Baseline (2014). Surprising Statistics About Big Data. Retrieved from https://www.smartdatacollective.com/what-is-future-of-business-intelligence-in-coming-years/ on 11th March 2021.

Confessore N. (2018). Analytica and Facebook: The Scandal and the Fallout So Far. Retrieved from https://www.nytimes.com/2018/04/04/us/politics/cambr idge-analytica-scandal-fallout.html on 4th March 2021.

Conrad A. (2021). The Future of Business Intelligence (BI) in 2021. Retrieved from https://www.selecthub.com/business-intelligence/future-of-bi/ on 11th March 2021.

Conrad A. 10 Critically Important Business Intelligence Software Features. SelectHub: Retrieved from https://www.selecthub.com/business-intelligence/critical-business-intelligence-features/ on 5th March 2021.

Exe Software. 7 Problems that Business Intelligence Can Solve for Your Business. Retrieved from https://www.exesoftware.ro/7-problems-business-intelligence-can-solve/ on 10th March 2021.

Flaks V. (2020). Five Business Problems You Can Solve With BI Tools. Retrieved from https://www.forbes.com/sites/forbestechcouncil/2020/0

3/25/five-business-problems-you-can-solve-with-bi-tools/?sh=58d8b8d27e0d on 9th March 2021.

De Groot J. (2020). What is the General Data Protection Regulation? Understanding & Complying with GDPR Requirements in 2019. Retrieved from https://digitalguardian.com/blog/what-gdpr-general-data-protection-regulation-understanding-and-complying-gdpr-data-protection on 4th March 2021.

Dickson B. (2020). What is deepfake? Retrieved from https://bdtechtalks.com/2020/09/04/what-is-deepfake/ on 4th March 2021.

Domo.com. Visualize: Data Visualization Tool | Domo. Retrieved from https://www.domo.com/business-intelligence/visualization on 9th March 2021.,

Durcevic S. (2019). Obtain Business Development With Data Intelligence Tools & Technologies. Retrieved from https://www.datapine.com/blog/data-intelligence-and-information-intelligence-tools/ on 2nd March 2021.

Gibbs S. (2015). Hackers can hijack Wi-Fi Hello Barbie to spy on your children. Retrieved from https://www.theguardian.com/technology/2015/nov/26/hackers-can-hijack-wi-fi-hello-barbie-to-spy-on-your-children on 4th March 2021.

Hendrickson M. (2017). Legal Questions About Your Online Content, Answered. Retrieved from https://www.dreamhost.com/blog/10-legal-questions-online-content-answered/ on 4th March 2021.

Hooda S. (2020) How Artificial Intelligence Will Revolutionize the Way Video Games are Developed. Retrieved from https://insidebigdata.com/2020/11/27/how-artificial-intelligence-will-revolutionize-the-way-video-games-are-developed/ on March 9th, 2021.

James M. (nd). What is the Future of Business Intelligence in the Coming Year? Retrieved from https://www.smartdatacollective.com/what-is-future-of-business-intelligence-in-coming-years/ on 8th March 2021.

Lambert B. (2016). R.I.P. The Age Of Trustworthy Voice Recordings: New Adobe Software Perfectly Mimics Anyone's Voice. Retrieved from https://www.feelguide.com/2016/11/06/r-i-p-age-trustworthy-voice-recordings-new-adobe-software-perfectly-mimics-the-human-voice/ on 4th March 2021.

O'Connor N. (2018). Reforming the U.S. Approach to Data Protection and Privacy. Retrieved from https://www.cfr.org/report/reforming-us-approach-data-protection on 6th March 2018.

Pratt M.K & Josh F. (2019, Oct. 16). What is business intelligence? Transforming data into business insights. CIA Africa: https://www.cio.com/article/2439504/business-intelligence-definition-and-solutions.html

http://www.baselinemag.com/analytics-big-data/slideshows/surprising-statistics-about-big-data.html

Rec faces (2020). How Accurate is Facial Recognition Today? Retrieved from https://recfaces.com/articles/how-accurate-is-facial-recognition on 10th March 2021.

Soderbag B. (2016). Persistent Transparency: Baltimore surveillance plane documents reveal ignored pleas to go public, who knew about the program, and differing opinions on privacy. Baltimore City Paper. Retrieved from https://www.baltimoresun.com/citypaper/bcp-110216-mobs-aerial-surveillance-20161101-story.html on 4th March 2021.

Solon O. (2017, Mar 9). With the latest WikiLeaks revelations about the CIA – is privacy really dead? The Guardian San Francisco Edition: Retrieved https://www.theguardian.com/world/2017/mar/09/with-the-latest-wikileaks-revelations-about-the-cia-is-privacy-really-dead on 4th March 2021.

Scheps S. (2008). Business Intelligence for Dummies. Wiley Publishing Inc.

Tableau. What is business intelligence? Your guide to BI and why it matters. Retrieved from https://www.tableau.com/learn/articles/business-intelligence on 4th March 2021.

Timothi G. (2017). Predictive Analytics – Facts You Must Know (Infographic). Retrieved from https://bloggingrepublic.com/predictive-analytics-facts-must-know/on 6th March 2021.

White D. K. et al (2020). Trajectories of Gait Speed Predict Mortality in Well-Functioning Older Adults: The Health, Aging, and Body Composition Study. The Journals of Gerontology: Series A, Volume 68, Issue 4, April 2013, Pages 456–464, https://doi.org/10.1093/gerona/gls197 Published: 09 October 2012

Index